Great Horned Owlets Rescue

Great Horned Owlets Rescue

WHERE THERE'S A WILL, THERE'S A WAY....

CHERYL AGUIAR

CONTENTS

DEDICATION

I DEDICATE THIS BOOK to my husband, James D. Aguiar Jr., who has shown me the true meaning of unconditional love. He has taught me that before you can truly love someone or something else in life, you must first love yourself. He stands by my side, encouraging me to chase my dreams and giving me the confidence to make them reality. Without him, I would not be the person I am today. He helped me find myself and the inner strengths I didn't even know I had, but most of all, he has taught me, to be... me.

ACKNOWLEDGMENTS

A SPECIAL THANK YOU to Mark Wilson for all his guidance and advice. To the Jacob family, the Ramos family and the Greenhalgh family, thank you for your help as the babysitters. Thank you to my parents, Tom and Arline Greenhalgh, for their help and support keeping me updated while I was at work; being my eyes while I was away. A big thank you to Celeste Soares and Sayra Flynn for their help with the final proofing. To Lori Pelletier and Jennifer Kirby for their help with the early stage proofreading. Lastly, a very special thank you to my husband Jim for standing by me, helping me with anything we needed to do. I am grateful for the way he understands my love and passion for all things wild and the wonder of nature. Jim is my life partner and truly my very best friend. I could not have done this without him. I will cherish this forever.

INTRODUCTION

MY LOVE FOR ANIMALS started from the moment my parents brought home our very first pet and continued to grow with every stage of my life. I always felt a strong connection and created an even stronger bond with every animal that touched my life. As a child, my favorite animals included horses, wolves, deer and rabbits. I dreamt of running with wild horses and imagined exploring the woods with wolves. As I grew older, my fascination with animals became my passion. My first encounter with a wild animal came after my aunt's cat had stolen a tiny, pink, furless newborn creature from a nest in her woods. I brought it home and began feeding it kitten formula with an eye dropper. I fed it for weeks, not knowing what kind of animal it was until its tiny ears started to take shape and brown fur started to appear. It was the most adorable little rabbit I had ever seen. I kept him in a box beside my bed and continued caring for him as he grew. A strong bond was created between us; he trusted me. During the night, he would squeak, cry and continuously scratch at his box until I picked him up. I had to hold him in my hand until he fell asleep. He would then stay calm and quiet all-night long. I was amazed how I would wake in the morning to find him still in the palm of my hand, unharmed. I guess my instincts kept me from squeezing him too hard while I slept. I could tell he felt safe with me. He truly believed I was his mother. That was when I realized how truly amazing Mother Nature could be.

Throughout the years, my love for wildlife continued to grow, along with many attempts at saving anything from small birds to tiny frogs. Some were successful, and some were not, but I always tried to give them a fighting chance. One of my favorite little friends was a small tree frog from my backyard. One Sunday afternoon, my husband Jim, accidentally ran over him with the lawn mower while cutting the grass. Normally, before Jim cut the grass, I would walk around the yard and do a frog check while picking up the large sticks and branches. This time, I was running behind; still finishing errands in the house. After Jim realized he had hit the frog and saw it was still alive, he came to get me right away. He knew if there was still a slight chance to save him, I would give it my all. I quickly ran outside to see the frog. He had lost two of his feet, half of his upper lip and one of his eyes had been severely damaged. He was in bad shape and bleeding profusely. I brought him into the house, cleaned up his wounds, made a nice bed for him in a box and hoped for the best. I began feeding him small insects with a pair of tweezers. Within a couple of weeks, his mouth healed but remained distorted, leaving a portion of his upper lip missing. He now had a huge hole in his upper lip which would make it difficult for him to eat. His eye healed over but still looked cloudy and dull. The most amazing thing was… his two feet grew back! They were not perfect, but they worked. They just looked a little funny, poor guy. I named him Lucky and continued hand feeding him crickets daily. He seemed to love crickets the best. Lucky then moved from his small box to a medium sized fish tank that became his home. He made a full recovery and thoroughly enjoyed play time, exploring the rooms in my house. I would set up barricades to keep him safe, and to keep him from getting lost. I was amazed by this little creatures' will to live and enjoyed him for many years… yes years, Lucky lived for almost four years. Truly one of Mother Nature's miracles.

Another great encounter with wildlife came with the return of the wild turkey to our local woods. I was fascinated by this large, clumsy yet charming bird. The first flock of turkeys to come through our yard will stay in my memory forever. It was a flock of six, very large male turkeys which are referred to as toms. They started hanging around my front porch, eating bread crumbs I had thrown outside for the animals. When I noticed how much they loved the bread, I started cutting up small pieces and making baggies just for them. The bread was a welcomed treat for them, but only given in small amounts. I had read it was not good for them to eat too much of it, so I fed them mostly cracked corn, which they loved just as much.

From the very first time I went out to feed them, I noticed they were not afraid of me. I would open my front door when I saw them in the yard and they would coming running over as fast as they could. I laughed at the funny way they would run with their heads high in the air, full of excitement. I would sit on my front porch while each one of them would come take a piece of bread right from my hand. Soon, they started looking for me when I didn't come outside right away. They would walk up onto my porch, waiting at my door until I came out. Each one of them had their own personality. I named all of them and became very fond of them. They seemed to like me too. They thought of me as one of them, although I was certainly aware of the dangers of wild turkeys. These birds never showed aggression towards me at all. They even loved to show me their elaborate tail feathers by puffing up and strutting around in front of me. I would walk with them, talk with them and just thoroughly enjoyed watching them. They almost seemed to talk back to me with the different sounds they would make. I enjoyed them for many years until the flock started slowly dissipating. My friends were getting older. After a few years, I didn't see any of my friends from that flock anymore but continued making new friends with every new year. The new turkeys would take bread from my hand, but it was much harder to gain their trust. I never created the same bond with them as I had developed with my first six feathered friends. I will never forget them.

One of my biggest dreams came true a few years back when I had the opportunity to meet a full-blooded wolf face to face at a wolf program in a nearby city. My mother and I attended the program after my husband Jim surprised us by arranging tickets to be held at the door. We were unaware of what kind of event we were attending until we arrived. Jim, knowing how much I loved wolves, knew I would be so excited, but not even he knew we would get the chance to meet one. To look into the eyes of a real wolf was one of the most amazing experiences of my life. It was a feeling I could never explain in words. I instantly fell in love with this handsome one-hundred-and-fifty-pound black wolf named Zeab. He was truly a gentle giant.

Along with Zeab were two other ambassador wolves, Magpie and Abraham. The three of them were so beautiful; I was so touched by this experience. I began to sponsor Zeab and planned a visit to see him in Colorado. Zeab lives at Mission: Wolf in Westcliffe, Colorado, a sanctuary for wolves and wolf-dogs born into captivity that cannot be released back into the wild. The founder, Kent Weber's mission was to teach people about wolves and that wolves belong in the wild, not as pets. I supported his mission and was eager to visit the sanctuary. My dream was fulfilled again when Jim and I, along with my parents, made the trek to Colorado and spent the day at the sanctuary with Kent, his family of wolves and the volunteers that help run the sanctuary. We all got to spend some time with the wolves, as Kent shared a one on one with my family and I, at the sanctuary. I was able to experience the surreal feeling of looking into Zeab's eyes one more time. Being accepted by a wolf is again, a feeling I cannot explain. It does something to your soul. I thank Kent for allowing us this opportunity and teaching people everywhere just how amazing wolves really are. They are not the man-eating monsters that people make them out to be. They are truly amazing animals who rarely attack humans at all. I will continue to sponsor Zeab, the Mission: Wolf staff, volunteers and all the wolves that have been given a new chance at life. I hope to continue visiting them for years to come.

These are just a few of the many amazing experiences I have encountered by exploring the world of Mother Nature. This book is about my most recent experience with one of Mother Nature's most magnificent birds, the Great Horned Owl, also known as the tiger owl. This mysterious bird is one of the top predators in the raptor food chain. They are aggressive, powerful birds that fiercely protect their young. They have been known to attack humans that wander too close. The amazing will of this family proved otherwise.

This is the story of how I gained the trust of an owl family in their time of need, allowing me into their lives in the wild.

Never stop exploring...
with Mother Nature
by your side,
the possibilities are
endless.

1

The New Family

DURING THE WINTER OF 2016, my husband Jim and I had been hearing the beautiful, echoing hoots from a pair of owls somewhere in the woods surrounding our home. The hooting began in late December and continued through the month of January. Their sounds became much louder and more frequent by early February. Winter was now setting in and by mid-February had become extremely cold, snowy and blustery. We could tell the owls were close by, but the howling winds blowing through the trees muffled the sounds of their hoots making it very hard to pinpoint exactly which direction the sounds were coming from. Almost every night beginning at dusk, we would hear them communicating back and forth to each other. What a beautiful sound. We were not certain what breed these owls might be, but we were certainly eager to find out. We learned that the male owl's voice was much louder and deeper than the female's voice. You could certainly hear the difference. She had a much higher pitched hoot. Although their hoots were loud, they had a deep muffled sound to them at the same time. To describe this, I would say it sounded as if you were speaking loudly with your hand covering your mouth. Perhaps this was part of the owls' natural defense; they sounded as though they could have been anywhere in those woods. It would be extremely hard to find them.

Jim and I live on a wooded lot behind my parent's home, in the neighborhood where I grew up. Having lived there most of my life, I had never heard owls around there before. This was now the second winter season that we had heard them, but still had not been able to spot them. I tried several times to find the owls in our woods but soon found, it was like chasing a ghost. I figured there was not much chance I would ever see one of these owls, but we certainly enjoyed listening to their hoots at night. It was so great, just knowing they were close by.

On a Sunday morning in late March, I decided to search the tops of the trees with my binoculars. Their hoots were even more frequent now and seemed to be isolated. I knew they had to be nesting somewhere close. I looked up and down each tree until finally, I discovered a nest in one of the tallest pine trees in the woods behind our home. Almost at the top of an eighty-foot-tall pine tree, in a nest made of large sticks and branches, I saw the face of a Great Horned Owl staring back at me! I could not believe my eyes. I stood silent, staring through the binoculars in disbelief. It was the most beautiful and majestic owl, I had ever seen. I observed the owl over the next few days and began to wonder if this was a female, incubating eggs, as I never saw her leave the nest. "How did she eat?" I thought to myself. It didn't take long before I discovered that she was waiting patiently for her mate to bring her a fresh meal while she closely guarded the nest. Not only did we have a mother Great Horned Owl, but a papa too. A pair of owls, nesting right in our backyard! I continued watching them from afar in amazement. We were still hearing the echo of their hoots at night as they seemed to communicate to each other. Their sounds were even more special now that we knew the location of the nest and hopefully the arrival of a new baby owl. How amazing to have a Great Horned Owl family so close to home. I decided to name the pair Mama and Papa, hoping they would become parents soon. For now, I thoroughly enjoyed watching Mama just sit in her nest. She had the most beautiful, bright yellow eyes I had ever seen. She seemed to look right at me, even though we were so far away from each other. She never seemed bothered that I was watching her, but always knew exactly where I was. She would peek around the tree branch to look at me as I was watching her in absolute amazement. As our eyes met, we made a definite connection; I fell in love with her.

As the weeks past, my wish came true. I noticed a little fluffy white owlet sitting in front of Mama in the nest. I was not exactly sure when the owlet hatched, but after looking back at my first photographs taken in late March, I saw the small puff in front of Mama's face in a picture that I had not noticed previously. She sure kept the little guy well-hidden. It must have hatched sometime before Easter and was much too small for me to notice, even with my binoculars, or the newborn may have been hiding under Mama to avoid the nasty weather.

A few days later, I noticed another little fluff in the nest! We now had two downy white owlets sitting eighty feet up in the swaying pine tree. These owlets looked like little white balls of fur with tiny black faces. They didn't even look like owls or at least not like any I had seen before. This was the first time I had ever seen a baby great horned owl and they were definitely not what I expected at all. They were so darn adorable!

The winter of 2016 would not let up; constant high winds, snow and freezing rain continued to make the family of great horns struggle to survive. I went out to check on them every day. I would watch Mama's long ear tufts and feathers blow around in the wind. I became fascinated with these owls and began researching them. I learned that owls' tufts resemble ears but are actually just tufts of feathers on the top of their heads, not ears or horns as in their name. Owls' ears are located on the sides of their heads, behind their eyes. The true purpose of these feathers is unknown; however, there are many hypotheses about the tufts. Some say they are used to scare away predators as the tuft feathers will stand straight up when the owl is alarmed by danger, while others say they are used as species

3

recognition so other owls can recognize them as one of their own. Another thought is for camouflage; the tufts along with the owls' brown colors will make their silhouette appear as a broken branch if the need to hide from predators should arise. Whichever is correct, I think the tuft feathers make an everlasting impression and give a unique look to the Great Horned Owl. It shows the majestic beauty and strength of these amazing birds. Mother Nature certainly knew what she was doing; they are a perfect fit, even when blowing over in the wind.

I felt so bad for this family. Not only was it extremely windy, but New England decided we should have a winter snow storm in April! Now, the family had to sit in a cold, wet and snow-covered nest. Mama never seemed bothered by this weather, but it certainly bothered me. I was sick with worry. "They must be so cold up there." I thought, "I Know, owls can adapt to any weather, they are wild, and this is nature." This was something I would have to keep telling myself... continuously.

Mama in the original nest with a little white owlet sitting below her eye.
Mama's ear tufts blowing over from the wind.

Photograph by Cheryl Aguiar.

5

The parents were becoming very busy working to feed and protect the family. Mama was always so cautious, landing on nearby tree branches, checking for predators before entering the nest. I would watch her land on the branch right by the nest, look around in every direction, then slowly side-step down the branch into the nest; trying not to draw attention to her little owlets inside. This was where I got my first look at her enormous foot talons (claws), they were massive. I quickly understood her rank in the food chain. I tried to remain very still when she returned so I would not alarm her, even though she still didn't seem to mind that I was watching her. I would stay far enough away from the nest, so I would not cause her to feel threatened. Binoculars and a great camera lens made it possible to watch and photograph her safely in a way that would not frighten her or interfere with her motherly duties.

The bad weather continued and was still a problem for this owl family. Mama sat high up in the tree top while it swayed back and forth from the heavy wind and rain. "Would this weather ever stop?" I thought, "They had it rough up there." The bad weather certainly makes it harder for owls to find food, which was extremely important with little owlets in the nest. Owls rely on sight and sound to find their prey, so heavy rains and high winds make it difficult to hear and locate a meal. I would see Papa fly in to meet Mama in a nearby tree to deliver food, then Mama would bring it to the owlets in the nest. At first, Mama did not stay away from the nest for very long. She would retrieve the meal and quickly return to the nest, but as time went on, I noticed her leaving for longer periods of time. I would sometimes get nervous for the owlets alone in the nest. Hawks would often circle high above the nest when she was gone. I always hoped she would return soon, but I knew she probably needed to help Papa find a meal for the family. These little guys were growing quick and were always hungry. Thankfully, she would always come back delivering a great meal.

By now, both parents had the duties of hunting for prey. The owlets needed to eat several times a day, and food was not always available. These owls feed on many small animals like snakes, rats, mice, rabbits, squirrels and many more, but can also eat larger animals such as skunks, ducks, geese and even hawks. They have been known to take down prey larger and heavier than themselves. Whatever it takes to feed their family. They were a team, working extremely hard to raise these little owlets. Owls are usually nocturnal hunters, but we saw both parents bring food to the nest in broad daylight. I noticed that Mama would return to the nest just before dark each night. I'm sure she continued hunting and feeding throughout the night, but I always felt better after seeing her return; just knowing she was close by. It was that time every night, that I too, would return to my nest. I was so happy to be able to witness a Great Horned Owl family living in our woods. At ease, I could sleep well and have pleasant dreams… Hoot… Hoot.

Mama sitting in the original nest. Photograph by Cheryl Aguiar.

7

2

The Rescue

ON THE EVENING of Thursday, April 21st, I went to check on the owl family as I did every night. As I looked up with my binoculars, to my dismay, I did not see the nest in the tree. I looked up again thinking I may have focused on the wrong tree, but it was gone. No nest and no owls. I stood there for a moment in bewilderment and disbelief. I had just seen them that morning. The nest was there, and they were all in it before I left for work. "What could possibly have happened to them while I was gone?" I thought. I decided to walk over to the bottom of the tree, which was something I had not done before. I always tried to stay as far away from them as possible. As I approached the tree, looking for the fallen nest, I found only a broken egg shell and a couple of pellets. Pellets are the undigested fur and bones of whatever the owl had previously eaten. Owls cannot digest the bones, fur or feathers from their prey, so after several hours, they discard it by regurgitating. In other words, throwing it up, much like a cat does with a fur ball.

I continued to search but saw no sign of the nest anywhere. I could not believe what I was seeing. The beautiful owl family was gone. I just stood at the base of the tree for a few moments looking around. I couldn't even find a branch or stick that looked like it might have belonged to the nest. My best guess was that the nest had fallen apart due to the extreme high winds we were experiencing. I discovered later, by looking back at earlier pictures, that the nest had been slowly deteriorating as time went on. This was most likely caused by all the activity from the little owlets jumping around, combined with the high winds, and not to mention; owls are terrible nest builders to begin with. In fact, they don't build nests at all. This nest had been up in the tree for several years and was well used by a family of hawks. Owls will take over a vacant nest before building one of their own. They obviously did not do a great job with the renovations on this one. I had such an empty, helpless feeling inside. "How could this happen?", I thought. It was so upsetting.

After a few minutes, I spotted one of the small owlets a good distance away from the tree where the nest once was. At the same time, my neighbor (who also checked on them daily) had joined me in the woods with the same concerns of the whereabouts of the nest. She had also spotted the same small owlet on the ground looking so frightened. We approached the little guy to check if he might be hurt. He instantly puffed up his wings in what is called defense mode, which makes them appear much larger. They do this, hoping to scare off predators. He appeared to be unharmed, but he was so young. We knew there were two owlets in the nest, so after more searching, we located the other one about twenty feet away. We also saw Mama watching from a nearby tree. She knew exactly where her owlets were, but we wondered if she would be able to protect them on the ground.

Soon, we were joined by my neighbors' husband and son. We all discussed how we should handle this situation. Should we put them in a box? Should we call someone? Mama was still there, so we did not want to take them away from her. If we had not seen Mama, we may have thought she abandoned them, but that was not the case.

9

She was very attentive. My neighbor's husband decided to try making some phone calls to wildlife professionals for advice. After several unsuccessful attempts to reach someone for help, he finally received one returned phone call. The advice from the professional was… "If the owlets are not injured or abandoned, then let Mother Nature take its course; leave them in the woods." Although I agree with that in most cases, this did not feel right to me. I knew the owlets were not injured, and yes, we did see Mama in a nearby tree, but these owls were so small. Anyone could see they were not ready to be out of the nest. They looked petrified to be on the ground in these big and dangerous woods; and they should be! They would be an easy meal for anything that night. They were way too young. Reluctantly, we left them alone and went back to our homes. I was very unhappy with the decision to leave them in the woods. If they had been a little older, bigger and stronger; I could see letting them be, but they were so small, so scared and my fear of a coyote, fox or even a neighborhood cat getting a hold of them was killing me. They were way too vulnerable. I could not leave them to die. Nor would I ever sleep that night.

Fortunately, my parents had attended a live owl program at the local high school about a month prior to this night. My mother suggested I give them a call for some advice. Agreeing that was a great suggestion, I made the phone call to Eyes On Owls in Dunstable, Massachusetts, an educational enterprise that cares for permanently disabled and injured owls. I left a detailed message about the owls and my concerns. That turned out to be the best decision I had ever made. Mark, who founded the program with his wife Marcia, called me back as soon as he could, agreeing with my decision; we had to get them off the ground. They were too young to defend themselves from predators on the ground. They would be eaten up for sure. It was getting very late by now, but Mark suggested this be done as soon as possible, since most predators hunt at night. They most likely would not have survived. He suggested building the owl family a new nest, attaching it to the same tree the original nest had fallen from. This was the only way to safely get the owlets off the ground and out of reach from harm's way. After telling him we were certain Mama was still around, he was hopeful that the parents would accept the new nest and continue to care for the little owlets. If they did not return, we would have to take a new action to help the little guys. Mark informed me that this was not to be taken lightly; Great Horned Owls can be very aggressive, especially when it comes to their babies. He informed me on how to properly handle this situation while protecting myself from possible injury. He also thanked me for having the courage to make such a dangerous attempt. As I hung up with Mark, my husband could already tell by my face, we had a project to do and quick! With the advice from Mark, Jim and I grabbed a wicker basket from my closet, grabbed a ladder, hard hat, gloves and made our way back into the woods. It was now dark; we had to use flashlights to search for the little ones in the woods. While I was locating the first one, Jim secured the wicker basket about twelve to thirteen feet up, on the same tree that the original nest had fallen from. That was as high as we could get it, given the circumstances. We had to act fast.

I found one of the owlets not far from where I had first discovered him. He appeared so frightened and stood as still as a stone. He had no idea what I was or what I was going to do to him. The poor little owlet didn't even fight me as I picked him up and held him close, reassuring my concerns that something else could have snatched him up in a heartbeat.

We could hear Mama hooting in the trees above us. That's where the hard hat came in… oh, did I mention the broom? Mark informed me that an owls flight is completely silent, I would never hear her flying at me. The strike from an owl can cause serious or permanent injury. He suggested one of us carry a broom, just in case Mama decided to attack me for taking her little ones. We certainly would not have hit her with the broom, just shooed her off if necessary. The hard hat would have protected my head from her massive talons; she could sink those talons into my skull in an instant. Knowing all of this could happen, I still had to try.

11

In the distance, we heard another hoot, coming from a different direction; Papa was there too. He was much farther away but hooted to let us know he wasn't too far and had his eyes on us. We had to be very careful handling their babies. Mama was staying much closer; she stood on a nearby branch watching our every move but did not attack. Maybe she sensed we were there to help. Perhaps she recognized me as we made eye contact every day since late March. Whatever the reason, I was grateful she let us help save her family. I climbed up the ladder with the first owlet in my arms and placed him in the nest. He instantly ducked down hiding in the basket but looked as though he felt safer already. I climbed down the ladder and headed back out to search for the other one, still hiding somewhere in the woods. My father had now arrived to help, bringing more lights to continue the search for the second owlet. I could still hear their parents in the trees, but so far, they were staying away. Finally, I found the second one, sitting behind a tree at the edge of a small murky pond of water. This made it a little tougher to rescue him. Just like his sibling earlier, he stood perfectly still. I had to reach around the tree, stepping into the water to reach him. He had somehow managed to get himself tangled up in some briars. After freeing him, I was able to pull him from the water. He was a little wet and muddy but gave me no trouble picking him up. Maybe he also sensed we were there to help. I held him close while my dad shined a flashlight for us to make our way safely through the dark woods to the new nest. In the meantime, Jim had run back to the house for more materials to secure the nest properly. As we waited for Jim to finish, my mom, aunt (in their pajamas!) and uncle had joined us to see if we needed help. They were able to meet the second little guy before I put him in the basket. He was so adorable.

After securing the new nest, Jim came down the ladder with good news that the first owlet was doing great but kept clapping his beak and hissing at him as he adjusted the basket. The poor little guy probably thought the nest was falling again. He was probably thinking, "Oh no, not again!"

I then carried the second owlet up the ladder and placed him into the basket with his sibling. They instantly snuggled together as I assured them they were now safe; they had a new home. "Success!" I thought, "The parents let us save their babies!" As I climbed down the ladder, I looked up at the basket and saw one of them peeking over the edge at us. Still looking a little frightened, I reassured him "Your Mama will be here soon." Well, I sure hoped she would. We quickly cleaned up and left the woods. I was keeping my fingers crossed, hoping the parents would come back, accept the new nest and continue caring for their little ones. What an amazing thing we had just done. What a great feeling it was thinking, we may have saved their lives. When we returned home that night, we sat on the couch, hoping we had done the right thing. Then about an hour later, we heard Mama and Papa's echoing hoots in the back woods. We instantly felt a great sense of relief and wondered if their hoots were a thank you for saving their family and creating a safe nest for their little owlets... Maybe :)

One of the owlets looking out after being placed in the new nest.

Photograph by Cheryl Aguiar.

3

The New Beginning

EARLY THE NEXT MORNING, I went out to check on them, hoping they were still there. I was so excited to see the two of them were cuddled up in the basket. They seemed to love it. I was soon greeted by my neighbor, who said she had seen people with hard hats in the woods that night and thought we called professionals to come help. She had no idea it was us in the woods. She was watching us unknowingly from her window, just so excited the owlets were being rescued. Now, she had the best view of the new nest from her kitchen window. She quickly informed me that Mama had come first thing that morning with something really big for breakfast. We could not have been happier. It worked! The owlets loved their new nest, and it appeared that Mama liked it too. Now, her babies have a better chance at growing bigger and stronger, with less worry of predators on the ground. However, raccoons could still climb the tree to ambush the nest. Mark had warned me that raccoons could still be a threat to the little ones, but I had not seen one in our neighborhood in quite some time. Besides, I was sure Mama could handle that! I just hoped they would stay safe. My neighbors were now deemed the full-time babysitters. It was comforting to know someone was checking on them throughout the day. My aunt, uncle and parents were always watching them too. They all knew to call me if anything happened while I wasn't there.

Sadly, I did not have a good view from my house, but I went out first thing every morning and night to check on them. I couldn't wait to get home from work; they were all I could think about. Luckily, their parents continued to care for them day and night. We just watched over them to make sure all was going well. With the cold, windy weather of winter still lingering; I now felt certain they would be safe and warm. Owlets are covered in a very thick, fluffy, grey and white down which keeps them extremely warm during the cold winter months. This is one of the reasons owls have their young in the dead of winter; the owlets would overheat in the warmer spring and summer months.

I soon began noticing a difference in the colors and personalities of the two siblings. I was not able to tell whether they were male or female, so I came up with what I thought was two suitable names. One was darker grey in color, larger and seemed to always stand tall and strong. He appeared to look after and protect his smaller sibling. This one likely hatched about a week before the other. When I first placed the two of them in the basket, this one was clapping his beak (clapping their beaks is meant to scare off predators) and peeking over the edge at us while the other one hid down inside. I named this one Wisdom. The other one was smaller in size, yet had a little more down around his face, making his face appear fuller and rounder. This one was slightly lighter in color and seemed to be very timid; never making much noise. He was always ducking down in the basket, hiding or laying low. Sometimes, I would arrive in the morning to see just one of them sitting in the basket. My heart would sink thinking, "Oh no! Where did he go? Did something happen overnight?" Then, he would pop up looking all messy and sleepy. I would let out a big sigh and think, "Oh thank goodness, he was just hiding... again." Most of the time, this one would be snuggled up against the larger sibling. I called this one Willow.

16

Willow snuggled up against Wisdom as he keeps guard.

Photograph by Cheryl Aguiar.

Enjoying the basket nest.

Photograph by Cheryl Aguiar.

Still reporting our progress to Mark, he suggested the next step was to support the bottom of the basket, now that we knew they were going to stay. Soon, they would start flapping their wings and jumping around to exercise. The basket needed to be secure enough to support their weight as they grew bigger and became heavier. Heavy rains could also weaken the bottom of the basket making it less secure. So, it was back to the drawing board. Jim designed and built a wooden platform to fit perfectly underneath the basket. This would also mean, hard hats on again and fingers crossed that Mama would allow us to get close to her owlets, once again.

Surprisingly, we had no trouble at all. Like the first time, Mama just sat up in the tree, watching and hooting to let us know she was well aware of what we were doing. Again, she did not attack. I would like to think she understood we were not a threat, but there to help them. The little guys did well too, Wisdom peeked over the edge at Jim, hissing only once. He had to protect little Willow of course, who just hid as usual. After a few minutes, they both seemed fine with Jim and let him secure the platform. "Thank goodness" I thought, "Another success!" Mama knew what was going on, yet she allowed us to help again. Now, the basket was more secure and sturdy enough for her to sit with her babies while feeding. The platform worked great; my neighbors said they saw Mama test the strength of the basket by stomping on the edge with her foot. Once she noticed it was more stable, she jumped inside. How amazing! Before we reinforced the basket, she would not get inside with the owlets, she would stand on the outside edge. She must have felt it wasn't sturdy enough and was not willing to take the risk. I was learning quickly that these birds were very smart… so very smart!

Owlet peeking through the handle hole after the new platform had
been attached underneath the basket.

Photograph by Cheryl Aguiar.

4

Week One

ONE WEEK HAD PASSED, and the owlets were growing like crazy! We were fascinated by how much we were learning about their personalities and behaviors. We were witnessing them just how they would have behaved in the wild, if their nest had not fallen from the tree top. It seemed as though they just picked up where they left off. They did not seem to be affected by the traumatic experience they had encountered just one week prior; it was amazing how well they adapted. They playfully pecked at each other, groomed each other and just seemed to enjoy cuddling up against each other. They had a definite bond; this was clear to see. It was life as usual for these little guys... eat, sleep and poop. We also discovered that young owls try not to mess in their nest. I was so amazed by this; they would lift their little rear ends up and stick them over the edge of the basket to poop. The first time I witnessed this, I thought the little guy was falling out of the nest, backwards! I said "Oh no! What are you doing? You are going to fall out!" I then realized, he was just pooping. He knew exactly what he was doing. We could see the white mess all over the sides of the basket and running down the tree. I wondered if owls did this, so they wouldn't fill their nests with poop. After all, they had to sleep in there. Who wants to sleep in their own mess?

This chalky, white stuff is called white wash. It is a uric acid produced by the kidneys that forms into a thick, white paste. It is the equivalent to urine in other mammals. The white wash will cover the sides of trees as well as plants and shrubs below, on the ground. It is normally present where owls nest or roost often and can be a good indication there might be an owl sitting up in the tree. So, if you see it, look up… but be careful!

The owlets were becoming youngsters in such a short time. I swore they were growing bigger every day. They were starting to lose some of that fluffy down, and those beautiful flight feathers were starting to show. They would occasionally stretch out their wings as far as they could; which showed how big they really were. The wingspan on these little guys, blew me away. An adult's wingspan can range from three to five feet, and with females slightly larger, possibly even six feet. These youngsters weren't far from that already!

Photography is another passion of mine, so I thoroughly enjoyed taking pictures of them in the basket nest. It would seem as though they were posing for the camera. Wisdom always sitting taller and Willow just relaxing. They were so darn cute. They appeared to enjoy their time in the basket nest, you could see they were comfortable and felt safe. I was so excited, yet always nervous to check on them each day and night; you never know what can happen. Each day was a wonderful gift. I was so surprised at how well this was working. At first, we were not even sure they would stay in the basket, let alone the parents would accept the nest and continue caring for them. I was truly amazed at how well the whole family adapted to this wicker basket nest. The young owls would not have had this chance if we had left them in the woods alone that night. Things were proceeding just as nature intended.

Wisdom standing guard while Willow takes a nap.

Photograph by Cheryl Aguiar.

Willow and Wisdom showing their personalities. Wisdom the protector and Willow's timid peek.

Photograph by Cheryl Aguiar.

We knew that soon, they would need to start exercising their wings and strengthening their legs. I was a little nervous for this stage, hoping they wouldn't fall. This is normally when they start venturing out onto the surrounding branches. Unfortunately, they didn't have any large branches around them like they did up in the original nest. There was only one branch above the basket nest and I was not sure they would be brave enough to use it. Jim saw this branch when he picked a spot for the basket, but like always, I needed to be sure they would have plenty of branches; not just one.

Mark suggested making a branch using a two by four piece of wood for them to climb on. So, Jim knowing I would not sleep until they had one, made a makeshift branch. We wrapped the ends with brown towels for grip. The smooth, bare wood might have been too hard for them to grip with their talons. We certainly didn't want them to fall off. This would mean, one more trip to the basket. As we approached the nest carrying the new branch, we saw Mama sitting in a nearby tree. We hoped she would allow us near the nest again. Before we started, I said hello to her and explained what we were doing. Of course, I knew she couldn't understand, but it made me feel better. She did not appear angry or disturbed but was very attentive. She stood on the branch, watching our every move as Jim attached the wooden branch to the bottom of the platform underneath the basket. I now felt confident, we had gained her trust. At first, the owlets both ducked inside the basket. Then, to my surprise, little Willow decided to check things out! He was still unsure and looked a little leery, but quickly peeked over the edge at us. Wisdom ducked inside, peeking out the hole from the basket handle. It wasn't long before Wisdom stood up to take his usual protective stance. He didn't hiss at Jim this time, just gave that strong, brave stare. We were able to attach the new branches quickly and had no trouble from any of them. We cleaned up and headed out. I turned back to say goodnight and saw the two of them just staring back at us. I wondered what they were thinking... did they know? Either way, I was just so happy to help them, and I could only hope they would learn to use them. They were so, so adorable. With the new branches in place, I could sleep once again.

Wisdom peeks over after the wood branches were attached.

Photograph by Cheryl Aguiar.

The new wood branches.

Photograph by Cheryl Aguiar.

5

Week Two

THE SECOND WEEK was terrible for Wisdom and Willow. The weather was just awful. It rained heavily for days and days without many breaks at all. They didn't seem to like this cold, wet weather; they looked so unhappy. The poor little guys stayed crouched down in the basket most of the time. Wisdom would be the brave one and sit up for a while, checking to see if Mama was coming soon, while Willow just hid, trying to avoid the soaking rain drops. Even though the owlets were covered in that thick fluffy down, the rain saturated their feathers; flattening their fluff completely. They were soaking wet. The look on their little faces saddened me, but I couldn't help but laugh a little, as they both resembled a soaking wet cat after an unwanted bath :(

Owl feathers are not waterproof like many other birds' feathers. They do not contain the oils that make feathers waterproof, which in turn, makes the owls' feathers lighter; enabling them to fly virtually silently. Their feathers are uniquely designed with comb-like ends, so the air flows through without turbulence. This enables the owl to flap its wings without making the usual gushing noise you hear when other birds fly. You cannot hear an owl flying through the trees; they are completely silent. Owls are the only birds able to fly with such stealth. This is how they surprise their prey and capture a meal for their family. The downside to this amazing feature is, not being waterproof. Owls will become heavy and soaked by the rain. This makes it difficult to fly and difficult to hunt. The sound of the rain also makes it harder to hear prey on the ground. These outcomes can be tragic for some owls and can even cause death by starvation. I hoped the rain would not last long enough to cause these kinds of problems for this family.

Mama and Papa appeared to be handling the weather just fine. It was the little ones that I was concerned with. I was already thinking to myself, "Hmmm, how can we put a roof over them?" Jim knew the look on my face and replied to me, "This is how they learn survival." He said, "There are no roofs in trees! It's nature." I knew this of course, but sometimes, I just can't help it… my heart takes over my mind. So, I then agreed, "Ok, no roof." This is when I had to remind myself… again, "They are wild birds, they know what they are doing!"

After the rain finally stopped, I wondered if they would ever be fluffy again. It didn't take long for their soaked feathers to dry up. Nature is so amazing… the downy fluff came right back! Although, I did notice something was a little different about the two of them; their stripes appeared darker. I wondered if the soaking rain caused them to lose some of their fluffy down, making their darker markings show more distinctly. They were definitely beginning to change. By this time, they were catching up in size and only slightly different in color. It was getting tougher to distinguish the difference between them however, I could still tell them apart, their personalities were still so very different.

Wisdom soaked from the rain. Little Willow is ducking down near Wisdom.

Photograph by Cheryl Aguiar.

The parents continued caring for the owlets as they grew into youngsters. They spent all their time hunting, feeding and protecting their little ones; they never stopped. We noticed hawks would sometimes circle the area above the trees screeching loudly, which sounded like a high-pitched scream. This was very, very disturbing! Wisdom and Willow would crouch down in the basket while all the neighbors made loud noises, trying to scare off the hawks, but that never seemed to work. Eventually, they would just fly off on their own. It was almost as though the hawks were trying to send a message. I'm not sure the reason for the threats, but luckily, they never attacked the little ones. We thought maybe the owl parents had taken one of the hawk's babies for food, and this was a warning for the parents to stay away. At this point, the owlets were far too large for the hawks to challenge anyway. The owlets' talons would scare away almost anything! I don't know what other predators came out during night, but I knew Mama and Papa would be on the case. They wouldn't let anything happen to their family. I'm sure, being nocturnal, they were much more active at night, working even harder to feed and protect them. Owls do most of their hunting at night, but even during the day, their jobs were never done. We saw them often, flying back and forth, delivering meals.

Two weeks had now passed, and I could not believe how much the owlets had grown. They were becoming young owls right before our eyes. They grew larger with every day. Their features and markings were becoming so much more visible. Wisdom was losing some of the grey down around his face which made him now appear lighter in color, while willow still had much of his down, making his face appear darker and rounder. I just loved to see how much they were changing, they were so beautiful. You could see the distinct colors and stripes of their flight feathers on their wings as they were becoming more like adults. Even their personalities changed in such a short time. They both stood with much more confidence. Willow was still a little timid but getting much better. We all spent so much time watching them. My neighbors told us they had binoculars at every window and a telescope for great viewing. They watched

Mama feed her little ones daily. We discussed how amazing this experience was and how all of us were focusing our concerns on making sure these little owls were safe. No one could wait to get home and check on them. Even while I was at work, my thoughts were always on them. I couldn't help but wonder, "Will they be in the basket when I get home? When will they leave?" and mostly, "Will they be okay when they do leave?" I didn't have any control over what would happen next, it was up to them. Owl parents continue to feed their youngsters throughout the summer and well into the fall, so I wondered if they would stay in the area around the nest. I hoped they would stay close by. How great it would be to watch them grow all summer long.

My neighbors invited me to take pictures from their back yard which had a much better view of the nest than from my house. I would normally take pictures from the edge of the woods behind my house which had lots of trees and branches in the way. I was able to capture some great photographs of our furry little friends from their view. The little guys seemed to like showing off their beautiful wings. Most times, I would be so fascinated by watching them, I would forget I had my camera. I just wanted to experience them with my own eyes. Those memories will stay in my mind forever. I fell deeply in love with these adorable creatures. Everyone was just so happy to be able to witness the success of the new wicker basket nest.

Wisdom shows off his beautiful wing feathers.

Photograph by Cheryl Aguiar.

Wisdom and Willow were both becoming more active, so much that I would get nervous they were going to fall out of the nest. This was so tough to watch. "I could not imagine being Mama", I thought, "She must worry all the time!" I knew if I was her, I would be a nervous wreck. They started flapping their wings vigorously, and quite often, much more than usual. It looked like they might try to fly out, but they just stayed in the basket, flapping away. Owls do this to gain strength in their wing muscles. What an amazing thing to witness. They also started standing on the edge of the basket. This also made me nervous, but they do this to gain balance and strength in their legs and feet. They were starting to become curious about the surroundings outside the basket too. You could see them looking all around, up and down. Wisdom noticed the branch high above the basket and I knew what was coming next. He jumped up onto the branch! Soon, they were both taking turns jumping up and down from the branch into the basket. I didn't even think they would use that branch. I was so proud of them. Jim knew exactly what he was doing when he placed the nest there. I was thrilled, but a little nervous for what was to come. We knew it wouldn't be long before they ventured farther outside the wicker basket. This was all happening so fast. Mother Nature wastes no time at all. They had almost doubled in size since we placed them in the basket nest. By this point, I don't think much of anything would try to approach them, I know I sure wouldn't. Look at the size of those talons... yikes!

Wisdom stands on the edge of the basket while Willow peeks from behind.

Photograph by Cheryl Aguiar.

6

The Time Has Come

ON FRIDAY, MAY 6th, Wisdom, the larger of the two jumped up to the high branch above the basket. He stood on the branch flapping his wings vigorously; gaining his balance as he stepped out farther and farther. He was becoming braver with each step. He had tried this before, but this time, he did not come back down. He stayed on that branch, looking out to the woods in front of him. I hoped Wisdom would stay practicing on that branch, then go back into the basket. Willow just stood on the edge of the basket, watching Wisdom. We knew the time was coming very soon, but they were still a little young to be venturing off. Even though they had grown much larger and stronger; they could not fly yet and were still quite vulnerable to predators on the ground. They would have to quickly run up a tree or hop fly up to a low branch to escape. I wondered if they would even know how to do this if they were faced with a predator. I knew their instincts would guide them, yet I still couldn't help but worry. I was a bit nervous to see what Wisdom would do next. This was all normal behavior for young owls, but as humans, we don't usually witness it. If he fell off, I just hoped he would stay close to the nest where it was safe.

I was able to capture this photograph of the two of them, who seemed to pose once again.

Wisdom sits on the branch while Willow sits on the edge of the basket.

Photograph by Cheryl Aguiar.

Just before dusk, I went back out to the woods to check on them. Willow had gone back into the basket, but Wisdom was still sitting up on the branch. I was a little worried, but they appeared to be content, so I returned home. That night, Jim and I decided to go out for dinner. As we were waiting to be seated, I received a phone call from my neighbor. He said one of the owls had fallen out of the nest. I knew right away, it had to be Wisdom. He must have decided to give flying a try and obviously, he failed. My neighbor said he nose-dived right to the ground. Jim knew I would not enjoy my meal, so we quickly left the restaurant and headed home. Our neighbors joined us in the woods to search for Wisdom. We all were concerned about him being on the ground. We soon found him sitting near a pile of rocks, not too far from the nest. He looked very frightened, so I carefully picked him up and held him close to me. My neighbors and I discussed how much these little owlets had taken over our lives for the time being. We could not stop worrying about them and couldn't wait to check on them once we arrived home each day. After a few moments, I carried him back to the basket nest. Willow was standing on the edge of basket, waiting patiently for his sibling to return. This time, there was no sign of Mama or Papa. I didn't hear them hooting in distance like usual. I put Wisdom back in the basket, hoping he would be safe for the night. I wondered if Mama and Papa were off hunting and didn't see what happened. I hoped they would return soon, but for now, Wisdom and Willow were safe again. We said goodnight and returned to our homes.

The next morning, I checked on them to find only Willow sitting in the nest. I looked around quickly but did not see Wisdom anywhere. As I returned to my yard, I spotted Wisdom sitting by the air conditioning unit on the back side of my house. This was definitely not a safe place for this little guy! He was out of the woods, heading straight for the front yard and the street. I decided to bring the youngster back to the woods once again. I could tell at this point he did not want to be in the nest, so I placed him on a tree branch near the nest. At least there, he would be safely off the ground and closer to his parents. He stayed there for a few minutes, then jumped down to the ground again. He ran over to a big pine tree, sat in front of it for a while, then disappeared off into the woods. I had such a sinking feeling in my stomach. My heart wanted to follow him, but I couldn't. I was already late for work and had to leave. That was a tough decision.

When I arrived home from work that evening, I went out to check on Willow, who was still sitting in the basket nest. He seemed to be content in the basket, unlike his anxious sibling who was eager to leave the nest. I started to search around for Wisdom. A few minutes later, my uncle came out offering to help find him. Together, we located Wisdom just over the fence in another neighbor's yard. At this point, it was so hard to decide what to do. I knew he was still too young and was not ready to fly. This was indeed a vulnerable time for him. He would have to flap climb up a tree if approached by a predator. I had not seen either of them even attempt that yet. I decided to call my neighbors (the full-time babysitters) for some advice. I really wanted to put him back near the nest where I knew he would be safe, but we all agreed, they were wild animals, and this is what they do. He obviously would have jumped out again anyway, and I could not protect them forever. I decided to leave him alone and let nature take its course. That night, I worried about him and hoped he would be okay. I felt sick, not knowing what happened to him. I could only hope that Mama had found him. As many nights in the past months, I did not sleep well at all....

Sunday morning came and no sight of Wisdom anywhere. I hoped he was okay and that I had made the right decision to leave him alone. We also had not seen Mama return to feed Willow, since Wisdom had left. He sat alone in the basket nest, waiting for food. It was so sad to see Willow sitting there, all alone. We did not know if the parents had come during the night, but there was no sight of them at all. My plan would be a trip to the nearby pet store to purchase some mice to feed Willow if Mama did not return soon.

Things changed later that afternoon. Willow jumped up to that high branch above the nest. He sat on the branch for quite some time, looking around until he built up enough courage to hop fly across to a tree branch away from the nest. We knew, he was about to make the journey away from the nest, just like his sibling Wisdom had done.

Willow on a branch after Wisdom had left.

Photograph by Cheryl Aguiar.

41

Willow waits, hoping his parents will come.

Photograph by Cheryl Aguiar.

Then right at dusk, Willow jumped down to the ground. He ran in the same direction as Wisdom had run the day before, but this time, I saw Mama come flying down. She landed on a tree branch across another neighbor's backyard at the edge of a larger patch of woods. She was calling out to Willow. This call was not her usual hoots, but a different squawking sound that I had not heard before. Willow ran through the woods but was having trouble getting over a wire fence between the yards. He heard Mama calling, then got a sudden burst of power and jumped up over the fence; running quickly across the grass to the woods where Mama was waiting. I was instantly consumed by an overwhelming feeling inside. I felt sad because he had left, but relieved that the youngster was with his mama. I then believed that his sibling, Wisdom, had done the same thing earlier and I could only hope he was in the woods waiting to greet Willow. I was still concerned about Wisdom; I wished I had seen him leave with Mama. Instead, I watched him run off alone. Maybe he felt he was ready to venture off on his own. Perhaps Wisdom's trip to my air conditioner before he left was to say goodbye… I'd sure like to think so anyway ;)

We had done everything we could do for this Great Horned Owl family. Now, it was up to the parents to do the rest. We do believe they coaxed the youngsters out of the basket early, taking them deeper into the woods where they could safely teach them to hunt, fly and become majestic adult owls. They may have stopped feeding Willow in the basket to coax him out of the nest to join them in the woods. Sometimes, owl parents stop feeding their young to force them out of the nest. The woods around the original nest may have become a concern for Mama to continue her duties as a parent. She had a greater plan. With the help of her mate, she did what she needed to do… take them to a more suitable place. I was so grateful we were able to give the owlets a chance to survive. They now had a much greater chance at becoming adults than when we first found them. I was still very concerned for them to be on the ground, but I knew that before long, they would be flying, and Mama and Papa would take great care of them. I hoped they would catch on fast.

I did not know where the parents would bring them, but I hoped they would stay close by. Owl families usually stick together until the babies are young adults which is almost a year. The parents will be very busy continuing to feed them over the next several months, until the youngsters are ready to find new territories and raise families of their own. We did the best we could do to help them get there. Still, I was very sad to see them go. I thoroughly enjoyed watching them and would miss them dearly. I envisioned that maybe I would see them flying around someday. That night, I could not stop the tears from falling. I had very mixed feelings about the way they had left. I laid in bed thinking of the whole experience over and over again. I could only hope that Wisdom and Willow would be okay. I then drifted off to sleep....

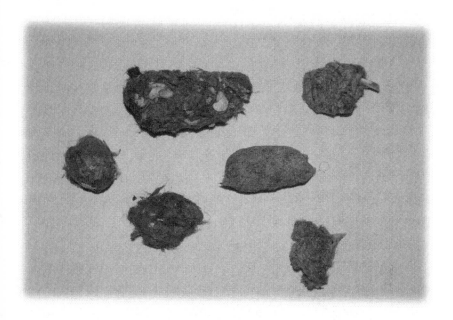

Pellets found around the wicker basket nest after Wisdom and Willow left with their parents. Owls cannot chew their food so larger prey are torn into smaller pieces and eaten, while smaller prey are swallowed whole. The fur and bones are undigested and regurgitated.

Photograph by Cheryl Aguiar.

7

The Gift

THE NEXT MORNING, I took a walk over to the basket, hoping maybe, they might still be around. I already knew, I would probably not see them again, but I needed to check anyway. Sadly, just as I expected... nothing. I glanced over at the empty nest in the tree and my eyes instantly filled with tears. I had grown so attached to these adorable, amazing birds in such a short time. They were all I could think about from the moment I saw them. I could not believe this was over already. My tears were filled with both sadness and joy at the same time. I was extremely sad they were gone, yet so happy we were successful in saving them, at least I hoped we were successful. I still didn't know what happened to them after they left. I hoped with all my heart that Wisdom and Willow were okay. I couldn't help but wonder, "Did Wisdom get lost before Mama could find him? Did they all meet up in the woods?" I knew that Willow was with Mama, but Wisdom? Oh, how I hoped they were all together.

Normally, young owls begin hop flying from branch to branch or at least know how to flap climb (flapping their wings while running up a tree) before leaving the nest area. Unless they did this during the night while we were sleeping, we only saw them venture out of the nest that one last day. Young owls usually practice this for weeks before they leave the nest. When they finally do leave the nest, it is called fledging. The owlets would then be referred to as fledglings. I don't think, "fledglings" was an appropriate name for these little guys yet, they were more like runaways! They left the nest a little earlier than they should have. This was the cause of my concern, with them away from the nest, they would have no safe haven. They would have to learn the ways of a fledgling and fast. Mama and Papa will have lots of work to do, feeding and protecting them.

I was certain Mama was grateful we helped save her little owlets, but at the same time, so much human interaction may have been what caused her to coax them away from the nest so early. They had lots of eyes watching them. Our entire neighborhood was watching them, and who could blame them? How often do you get to see owls so close to home? Even though everyone respected the family, the nest was close to the ground and highly visible. I'm sure that was not what Mama had planned for her family. I wondered if she waited until they were just old enough, then took them away to start their new life somewhere a little more secluded. I sure hoped that was what had happened to my friends.

For the next several days, I went out to the woods, hoping the family had come back, but still nothing... no hoots, no owls. Just the usual chirps of backyard birds filling the air with song. I would wait until dusk, then walk over to the fence at the edge of my aunt and uncle's yard where I had last seen them. That was the best view of the woods. Owls are most active at dusk, so I thought I might catch a glimpse of one of them, but as usual... nothing. Unfortunately, my aunt and uncle were away the night Willow left the wicker basket, so they did not get to say goodbye to our little friend. When they arrived home to see the empty nest, they were so disappointed. My aunt cried just like I had done earlier. We stood at the wooden fence overlooking the woods and cried again. I thought to myself, "We had done something so wonderful, why did my heart ache so much?" I think, I just needed to know they were safe. My aunt and uncle said I was more than welcome to come over to the fence and search their yard anytime and asked me to keep them updated. They too, hoped to see our little friends again. We already missed them so much.

For the next two weeks, I continued walking over to the fence, once in the morning and once again at dusk. Each time wishing, I might see my little friends again. After a while, reality was setting in and I was losing hope. They must have gone far away from the nest area. I was beginning to think, I would never see them again. I was grateful for the time I did get to spend with them, after all, seeing an owl in the wild is quite rare to begin with. I decided the next night, would be the last time I would go to the fence, hoping to see them. I couldn't do this forever, I was torturing myself. I returned home with a heartbroken feeling of sorrow.

The next day, I was feeling a little sad and uncertain about my decision to stop searching for them, so that night, I decided to try again. As I stood with my binoculars, looking at the empty trees, I was overcome by the feeling of an old memory; a vivid vision from my childhood. As a child, I loved to explore. In fact, I spent most of my childhood years, exploring the woods. My neighborhood had several small, murky ponds and streams where I would catch frogs and pollywogs in the summer and ice skate in the winter. I always had a great passion for nature and thoroughly enjoyed walking through the woods; sometimes for hours at a time. I have fond memories of that time, but for some strange reason, the memory of this one particular section of woods was so vivid. I felt like I was being drawn there. I decided to take a walk and visit this area. I remembered there being a path leading into the woods. I didn't think it would still be there, but much to my surprise, I could still see the original path I used as a child! It appeared to be well traveled by deer and many other animals... so cool. Luckily, I could still enter the path fairly easily. It was not over-grown yet despite being mid-May. The bad weather may have helped with that. As I entered the path, I took no more than five steps into the woods and heard a screeching sound. I stopped in my tracks to listen for a moment. I heard the screech again and knew in an instant, it had to be one of my little friends! I took a few more steps in and heard it again. I could not tell exactly where it was coming from, but I knew it was definitely an owl making that sound. It sounded a bit farther in, so I continued walking along the path when suddenly, I came across Mama sitting up on a tree branch. Now, I was sure it was the owls. I whispered with excitement, "Hi Mama, I'm so happy to see you!" Like before, Mama did not seem frightened by my presence at all, she just stood on the branch looking majestic and beautiful as always. Shortly after, I heard the screech again and knew it was one of the little guys somewhere in the ferns to the side of me. It sounded like he was on the ground, but I could not see him. This area of the woods had a murky stream with lots and lots of lush greenery everywhere. "What a perfect place to live." I thought, "If this was where they made their new home. They could definitely hide well and stay safe in here." Then, from the corner of my eye, I caught a glimpse of something moving in the thick greens on the ground. It was one of the little guys! I saw him for just a split second, then he quickly disappeared into the greens. I could not believe my eyes!

The new home by the stream.

Photograph by Cheryl Aguiar.

I was not sure if it was Wisdom or Willow hiding in the greens, but I was so excited. I didn't know whether I should stay in the woods or leave right away. I certainly did not want to frighten them. I decided not to stay for too long, but I wanted to know if both youngsters where there, so I looked around quickly, but was unsuccessful. I didn't hear or see the other one, so I said goodbye to Mama and made my way out of the woods. I didn't want to scare them or make them feel as though the woods was an unsafe place for them to live. Really, I could have stayed there forever! I was just so very happy to see them. Even though I did not see both young owls, I was hopeful that the whole family was still together.

When I returned home, I could not wait to tell Jim what I had seen. While I was waiting for him to come home from work, I sat thinking about what had just happened. "What on earth made me go to that particular area? Why did I have such a strong sense to go there?" I wondered, "Could it have been just a coincidence that they were right there when I walked into the woods?" The more I thought about it, the more I could not believe it. They could have been anywhere in those woods by now. We have acres and acres of woods surrounding us, how on earth did I know to go right there? I may never be able to explain that, but I felt something… something strong. I will leave it at that.

I started thinking, maybe the screech I heard when I entered the woods was his way of saying, "Hello step mom, I'm right here, and I am okay!" He could have remained completely silent, and I would never have known he was there, but he didn't. "Did he want me to find him?" I thought. "Maybe… Something sure encouraged me to go there… but why?"

When Jim arrived home, I barely waited for him to walk in the door before I started telling him what happened to me. He replied, "Did you really think they wouldn't let you know where they were and that they were okay? You are Pocahontas you know." – He always tells me I am Pocahontas. He believes I have a special way with animals both domestic and wild. He wasn't sure how, but he knew they would find some way to let me know they were safe and doing well.

I was so excited and could not wait to tell my family and neighbors how I had seen them. I told them how I saw only one of the youngsters, but I was hopeful they were both there. Everyone was just as thrilled as I, that they were safe. We all had done such a great job.

That night, I lied awake thinking of Wisdom and Willow. Maybe both siblings were there, and Willow, who was always the timid one, was just hiding or being shy as usual. My thoughts quickly turned to Wisdom, who I did not see leave with Mama that last night. The more I thought about him, the more I began to feel sad. I didn't know for sure, exactly what happened to him, so I tried to remain hopeful. It could have been either one of them in the woods. At least I knew Mama and one of the youngsters were together and safe. I told myself, "They both had to be there, I just didn't hear the second one." I had to stay positive.

The next day, I could not stop thinking about them. I couldn't help but wonder if both Wisdom and Willow were in those woods with Mama. It was eating me up inside that I had only heard one of them. I thought to myself, "What if Wisdom never found the rest of the family and something bad happened to him?" I started thinking back to the night Wisdom took off alone, "Should I have brought him back to his sibling to wait for Mama? Did I make the right decision to leave him alone? Why do I keep torturing myself?" I had to remind myself again… "They are wild animals and you did all you could. This is the way of nature." Even if the original nest had not fallen out of the tree, this would still have happened. They all leave the nest at some point, but I would not have been a part of it. For some reason, I was brought into this owl family's life… now they have become a part of mine. After thinking more about it, I made the decision to go see them again in a few days. I needed to know if Wisdom was all right. I needed to hear two screeches in that woods. There was a part of me that wouldn't rest until I did. If something bad did happen to him, I would certainly feel awful, but I knew there was nothing else I could have done. I tried my best, but not knowing, was eating me up inside. If only I could know for sure that both youngsters were there, I could then feel this was a complete success.

Three days later, I went back into the woods, instantly hearing the voice of one of the little owls. I couldn't see him, but he was there, hiding in the greens. Mama was sitting on a high branch watching over her youngster on the ground. I stood still, listening very closely but still heard only one screech. I was both happy and sad at the same time. I thought for sure, I would hear two of them. I looked up at Mama, who didn't seem to mind me watching them, so I decided to stay longer than the first time. I stood for a while, enjoying my friends, but sadly, I still did not hear a second screech. I thanked Mama for letting me visit again, said goodnight and returned home.

That night, I was so sad about not hearing the second little owl. I still didn't know which one of them was in the woods, but I was so worried it was Wisdom that did not make it. In the beginning, he was the one I would have bet on making it through anything, but now, I was not so sure. I guess I just felt it was Willow in the woods because I saw him leave with Mama. I couldn't be sure about Wisdom. I hoped he made it to the new home too. The basket nest kept them safe enough to get them to this point, they just had to make it all the way. If we had not provided them with the new nest, neither one of them would have survived long enough to make it this far. They would have been killed on the ground before even getting the chance to grow at all. At least I knew Mama had one of them with her. Thinking of this, I did not sleep well for the next few nights.

I waited a few more days before going back to the woods for another visit. I did not want to disturb the family too much. This time when I approached the woods, I did not see Mama sitting up in the tree. As I looked for her, I heard the screech from the little guy, somewhere near the stream. Then, I heard another screech, but this one was coming from the other side of the stream. I stopped right in my tracks and said "Wisdom, is that you?" Again, I heard one screech then another! It was definitely coming from two different directions. "Yay! Oh, my goodness... I hear two!" I thought, "My two little friends made it safely to the woods!" I could not begin to explain how happy this made me. I tried to locate them hiding beneath the layers of greenery, but it was much too thick, they stayed well hidden. At that point, I didn't even care that I could not see them; they were both there and safe. That was all that mattered. What a fantastic feeling; the rescue was a success. Both little ones found their way to Mama in the woods that night. Wisdom was most likely there waiting for Willow the whole time. I'm sure Mama knew exactly what she was doing. She waited until little Willow had enough courage to leave the nest and join them in the woods. She then guided the two of them to a quiet, secluded stream deep in the woods where she could raise her family. "Great job Mama!"

As I stood listening to the wonderful screeching sounds coming from underneath the bed of plants and trees, I looked around and soon realized that this was indeed the perfect place for the family to live. There must have been plenty of food sources from the murky stream and lots of places for the little owls to hide while they learned how to get off the ground. I wished I could see them, but the young owls were so well hidden. What a sense of relief to hear the two of them in that woods. A huge weight had been lifted off my shoulders. Before long, Mama came flying down, landing on a nearby branch. I told her what a great job she had done. I also thanked her for letting me know that both of her beautiful young owls were safe, and the family was together. Even though I still couldn't see them, just hearing them was all the proof I needed. I returned home to tell Jim the great news, both of my little friends were in the woods, and I had definitely heard the screech from both of them. Maybe Willow was being shy as usual until he got the nerve to speak up. Whatever the reason, I slept like a baby that night. My friends were all safe and sound in their new home.

I continued to visit them every few days. It soon became my new routine. I would come home from work, then head straight to the woods. When I arrived, I would see Mama, say hello, then listen to hear where Wisdom and Willow were hiding. These young owls were always on the move; they were never in the same place twice. I'm sure they were having a great time exploring their new home. I just loved to stay and listen to them screech to Mama, letting her know where they were. They were impossible to spot in the lush woods. Their screeches always came from the thick greenery covering the ground, leading me to believe they were not flying yet. They may have been hop flying from branch to branch in the low, smaller trees and plants but not venturing out too far, they remained hidden and safe.

On my next visit, while I was walking into the woods, I came across a small black rat lying dead, in the path which I used to reach them. It was freshly killed, but not eaten. I thought, "Oh, this must be a present to show me they are getting better at hunting. Great job guys. Maybe next time, you should try eating it!" I laughed and continued on to see my friends. I pictured Mama teaching them to catch the rat and them tossing it around with their beaks to get the idea of what to do with it. Although, I believe that the parents still do most of the hunting at this point, but who knows, it could have been the little guys. That also meant they were covering more ground, venturing out of the thick greens. They were getting to be brave young owls. The murky stream must have had lots of rats, frogs and other prey for them to practice their hunting skills. This must have been where Mama and Papa had gone to find food for feeding the owlets back when they were in the basket nest. We saw the parents bring black rats and snakes to the nest a few times. They probably captured most of their food from here.

When I arrived at the stream, I heard both of them screeching from the greens, but did not see them. I was hoping this time, they would be out of the greens and I would have a chance to see them, but... no chance, they were still not visible. I figured they were probably waiting to go back to the rat to finish what they had started, so I visited the family for only a few minutes then returned home. I wanted them to eat the rat while it was still fresh. How exciting!

Throughout the next couple of weeks, they continued to leave what I called presents, in the path each time I visited. Most of the time it was a soft, beautiful brown feather, just enough to let me know they were doing okay. Other times, it would be animal remains of some kind. I didn't mind the meal presents, but I liked the soft feathers much better. Who wouldn't?

One day, a few weeks later, I noticed an area of ferns deeper into the woods which was covered in white wash. I had not seen signs of white wash on those ferns before. The tops of the ferns had the most coverage which meant it was dropping from directly above. I looked up and saw a very large tree branch, stretching out above the ferns. I knew they must have been sitting up on that branch. That meant, they were finally off the ground! I looked for them in the surrounding trees but like usual, I could hear them, but could not see them. I couldn't believe how well they stayed camouflaged in those trees. They sounded like they were right in front of me, yet I just could not spot them. I was so excited to know they had begun to venture up, into the higher trees. I hoped that soon, I would be able to see them.

On my next visit, I heard Wisdom and Willow, but they sounded farther away than usual. As I looked around, I noticed a tree shaking in the distance. The tree was covered in bittersweet and something was in the bittersweet, causing it to shake. Suddenly, I caught a glimpse of wings, flapping vigorously at the top of the tree. I could tell by the color of the wings, it was not Mama, it was one of the little guys! He was hiding in the greens of course, even while sitting at the top of a tree. I tried to get a better look, but I could only see him when he flapped his wings. I then saw Mama fly overhead landing in the same bunch of trees. After seeing her, I knew for sure, it was one of them. I did not get a great look at him, but finally, I saw one. I visited for a while that night. Just watching the bittersweet shake in the tree was so exciting. That was all I saw of them that night, but I returned home with such a great feeling of excitement, they were all doing so well. I felt like a proud step mama…this was so amazing.

The next visit, I saw the bittersweet covered trees shaking again, so I decided I would stay a little longer than the night before. Then right at dusk, I spotted the two of them! They were not in the same tree, but close to each other. This was the first time I actually saw both of them together in these woods at the same time. They were

56

stretching their wings out and flapping vigorously to practice balancing on the tree limbs. I said, "Look at you guys!" I was so proud of them. Mama just stood on a nearby tree branch, watching over her little ones. Then suddenly, another wonderful surprise... Papa! I had not seen Papa since before they left the wicker basket nest. He flew over landing on a tree limb beside Mama. This was a fantastic gift... amazing. I finally saw the whole family together at last. I greeted Papa with much excitement. I stood in awe for a moment thinking, "I cannot believe this is happening. What a gift to be able to witness this entire Great Horned Owl family living in the wild. Why was I given such a special gift?" I believe it was Mama's way of thanking me for saving her two owlets and giving them a chance to become young adults. She allowed me to watch them grow and gave me peace knowing they were all safe and well. I was so grateful to her. I went home that night with a feeling of complete happiness, thinking "Life could not get any better than this." I also left with two more feathers to take home with me. I just loved the little gifts from my owl friends.

8

At Dusk

I DECIDED TO WAIT a little closer to dusk before going into the woods for my next visit. I thought their silhouettes might stand out amongst the leaves in the backlit sky while the sun was setting. The young owls would be more active and easier to spot in the thick, green covered trees. Then, just like I had hoped, Wisdom and Willow were high up in the trees, hop flying from branch to branch and tree to tree. They were certainly getting the hang of it, they were catching on fast. I was thinking to myself, "Look at them go, they were almost flying!" Most of the time, they would stick around the same few trees, they seemed to love this area they had found. The thick greenery surrounding the stream made a great place for them to hide while they were gaining their balance and strength, now they were venturing out higher and higher. They would have done this back in the woods near the original nest, if things had been normal and the nest had not fallen from the pine tree early on. They adapted so well to their new home in the woods.

That night, I was able to get a good look at them with the binoculars and thought, "Oh my, they were getting so big!" They still had a lot of downy feathers but had more detail in their face colors. I could see their facial disks, and the dark colored bars around their eyes much more distinctly. I could definitely see a change in the color of their chest feathers, and their wing and flight feathers were just beautiful. They were certainly beginning to resemble the adults, even though by looking at them, you could see they were still so young. They still had some fluffy down on their heads, and their tufts feathers had not quite grown in yet, making their heads appear very round. Their bodies now appeared to be about the same in color. The grey colored down had given way to beautiful shades of brown. It was hard to tell the difference in their size at this point, they were sitting too far away from one another. I was just thrilled to see that they had both become the beautiful young owls I had hoped for. It was an honor to watch them grow.

Over the next couple of visits, I continued to watch the entire family thrive. I soon figured out that if I heard crows squawking loudly when I arrived, it usually meant Mama had been up to no good. She must have been sneaking into other birds' nests, looking for a quick meal for the family. I often saw blue jays and crows dive-bombing Mama while she stood perched on a tree branch. I thought, "This must be a warning for Mama to stay away from their nests." The smaller birds would fly around, hitting her on the top of her head continuously. This harassing behavior from the other birds is called mobbing. They do this to warn off predators and protect their young. Most of the time, she would take it pretty well, but when she finally had enough, she would just fly off to another tree. It never seemed to bother her too much. Eventually, the smaller birds would just give up and fly away. I'm sure they thought they got their point across, but it never seemed to stop Mama; she never gave up. I saw this happen often... poor Mama.

One time, I came across another present while walking on the path. This time, it was not the usual fluffy brown and white feather presents I was used to finding, but a half-eaten foot from some kind of animal. Actually, it was a foot and part of a leg bone! It had grey fur (well, what was left of the fur) which was very wet looking. "Maybe, it's a water animal?" I thought. It was medium sized with huge claws. The foot was all that remained of whatever it was that I had stumbled upon. I walked a few more steps and saw a small piece of carrion, covered in beetles. They were carrion beetles. I had heard of these before but never actually saw them eating something. Gross! I then wondered if maybe, they finally made a kill of their own and left me a piece to show what they had accomplished. I thought, "Great job little ones! You got yourselves a meal!" I snapped a picture of the foot, so I could try to figure out what it was they had eaten.

Later that night, I did a little research and matched the remains I found, to that of a muskrat. Which made perfect sense, because the stream was the perfect habitat for a muskrat. I didn't know if it was Mama or the little guys who caught it, but I was still so proud of my little owl friends. They were doing great and hopefully, becoming hunters. I still preferred the feather gifts much better, but I was glad to see they were eating well. I wondered, "What gifts would I find next time?" I was kind of hoping for those beautiful brown feathers, at least I could bring those home with me. The meal leftovers always stayed in the woods!

The next time, as I entered the woods at dusk, I saw Wisdom and Willow almost immediately. As I stood watching, I heard a snapping noise coming from behind me. I knew it was the sound of sticks breaking, like someone or something was walking through the woods. It sounded close by, so I turned around very slowly. I reached for my pepper spray which I always carried with me while I was in the woods. Luckily, I had not had a reason to use it... yet. I was thinking, "Oh boy, please don't be something bad, I don't want to have to use this, I don't even know if it works!" As I turned around, I saw a very large, beautiful doe looking back at me! She wasn't more than fifteen feet away from where I was standing. I stood completely still, staring for a moment, then said hello to her. She also stood very still, staring back at me. She then continued slowly walking on her way through the woods. I was completely stunned for a moment and thought, "Wow, that was a deer. Did I really just see that?" I had to take a deep breath and savor that moment. She was absolutely beautiful. The owls were not the only ones living in these woods. I was so glad I got the chance to see her. The most amazing things happen when you spend time with Mother Nature. If you respect her, she allows you into her world. What an amazing feeling.

I then turned back and continued watching Wisdom and Willow as they flew from tree to tree. Then, for the first time, the two of them landed on a tree branch together. Until now, I would see both of them, but in different trees or on different branches, never together on the same branch. This was so great to see. They were pecking at each other playfully, like siblings do, just enjoying each other's company. This reminded me of when they were in the basket nest near my house. The two siblings still had a close bond just as they did before. I still had a little trouble telling them apart at this point. Even though they were close together they were too far away for me to make that distinction. Just seeing them sitting close together again was fine with me! I couldn't have asked for more. That was truly the best gift yet. The family was progressing exactly the way nature intended, with a little help from us to get them on their way.

My next visit was an interesting one, to say the least. I figured out that dusk seemed to be the best time for the owl family and I to enjoy our visits. I was just getting home from work, and the young owls were just starting to become active, waiting for Mama to begin her night time hunting. Even the deer made an appearance at that time. So, waiting until dusk, I went back to visit again, wondering what I would see this time.

I arrived to see my owl friends were doing great as usual. They were hanging out and flying through the trees when suddenly, one of them landed on a tree branch right in front of me! It was almost as if he wanted to say hello! He was a little off balance on his landing, so I chuckled a bit saying, "Oh, hello there little one... oh boy, hang on! Don't fall off!" He soon found his footing and stayed perched there for a few minutes, allowing me to get a close look at him this time; I believed this was little Willow. It was great to finally see him this close. I could now see how much he had grown. He was just beautiful. He then flew off to join Wisdom on a nearby tree branch.

As I stood watching the two of them, I heard something rustling in the leaves. It was under a patch of ferns near the edge of the stream. The tops of the ferns at the back of the patch were shaking. The shaking was getting closer, heading right in my direction. Something was underneath the ferns, moving quickly towards me. Once it reached me, it stopped. I looked down at my feet, and a raccoon peeked its head out from the ferns! The raccoon was just as stunned to see me as I was to see him. We just stood, staring at each other for a few seconds, then he started slowly back stepping into the ferns while keeping his eyes on me as if to say, "Ok, I'm going to back up real slow and maybe she will forget she saw me." He was so darn cute! He disappeared into the ferns and I thought for sure he must have run off, but I was wrong. He had climbed up a tree just a few feet in front of me. Now at eye level, he slowly peeked around the tree from side to side; he seemed very curious about me. His demeanor seemed to say, "What the heck are you, a big raccoon? I haven't seen one like you before!" He was actually quite comical. I chuckled as he continued to climb higher and higher, stopping every few feet to peek around the tree to see if I was still there. He then stopped at a large branch midway up the tree. He stood on the branch, wagging his tail, just looking at me. After a few minutes, he actually sat down! I thought, "Ok little buddy, you can watch me if you like." He seemed pretty comfortable up there, and I felt as though the raccoon was not a threat to me, just curious. He did not appear angry or disturbed, so I continued watching him and the owls. It was getting dark at that point, but so much was happening that I did not want to leave. I made a new raccoon friend while watching my owl friends! What could be better than that?

About twenty minutes had passed, and the raccoon was still perched up in the tree. I was looking up at the owls when I heard a strange, very loud sound coming from the greenery in front of me. I would describe this sound as a cross between a growl, a scream and a loud screech from a bird at the same time. I had never heard an animal sound like that before. Then suddenly, another scream, but much louder this time. The little raccoon jumped up in fear and ran down the tree, scurrying away. The sound had come from directly in front of me at the time, so I couldn't tell whether it was coming from across the stream or in the ferns at my feet, but I was not taking the chance to find out! I myself, turned around and ran as fast as I could. If the raccoon was frightened, then I knew this had to be something I would not want to encounter! I ran out of the woods and headed home. I was a little shaken up when I returned home. I told Jim what happened to me and my new raccoon friend in the woods. He knew something bad happened by the look on my face; I was pale when I walked into the house. He could tell, whatever just happened, it was not good! After explaining what I heard, we searched the internet for information on what kind of animal, that loud screeching sound could have come from. I soon learned, the sound I heard, matched the sound which comes from a fisher cat. I thought, "Oh my goodness, a fisher cat! Not only do I never want to meet up with him in the woods again, but the owls; the poor owls! I hope they are all okay!" I knew they were high up in those trees, but I wasn't sure just how high a fisher cat could climb. I hoped that the fisher cat did not try to attack them. I was sick with worry that night. Maybe life over there was not as easy as I thought. Even though adult owls have no serious predators, they can occasionally be caught off guard, and the youngsters may not be old enough to defend themselves yet. I hoped Mama had taught them enough to survive. I knew this probably wasn't the first time something threatening had ventured in to their territory. There were lots of predators around that the young owls needed to look out for in those woods and fisher cats were one of them. They can be extremely vicious animals and have been known to attack and eat other animals like… raccoons. I hoped that my little raccoon friend escaped unharmed that night as well. I don't think this was his first encounter with the fisher cat either. He certainly had the right idea… run!

By this time, I decided that going into the woods at dusk was no longer a good (or safe!) idea for me. Even carrying my pepper spray, a fisher cat was something I did not want to meet up with in those woods. I was comfortable with the deer, even the raccoon, but not the fisher cat. I decided from that day forward, I would try to visit them a little earlier, before dusk... way before dusk! All kinds of creatures come out at dusk, and I'm not sure I like some of them! Well, one in particular. Although, I completely understand he has his place in the food chain. After all, he is one of Mother Nature's creatures, I just hoped he didn't try to attack the owls.

The next morning, I awoke worrying about my friends in the woods. I needed to make sure the family was okay after the encounter with the fisher cat. Luckily, it was Sunday which meant I could go check on them much earlier than I could during the week. I had never visited them in the middle of the day before, so I was unsure if they would even be around. I've always heard that owls are rarely seen during the day; they are nocturnal and normally sleep during the daylight hours. However, I witnessed Mama and Papa bringing food during the day, several times at the original nest before it fell. In fact, they worked hard all day long feeding their young. I don't know when they slept, if they did at all!

I decided I would go check on them around 2:30 in the afternoon. When I arrived, I entered the woods with extreme caution; I was still a bit leery from the previous night's encounter. I wasn't sure what I would find when I arrived. I wondered, "Did they fight with the fisher cat? Would there be feathers everywhere or fur everywhere?" The fisher cat might be a vicious animal, but the Great Horned Owl can be a just as tough. I'm not sure which one would win that battle.

After making it to the stream safely, I was both pleasantly surprised and extremely relieved to see Wisdom and Willow snuggled up together on a high tree branch. They were both safe and sound. Thank goodness, the fisher cat did not attack my little friends. I was overcome with joy and relief. Not only were they safe, but they were highly visible, in the middle of the day! How cool to be able to see this. It was an extremely windy day, being early June. The poor little guys looked like they were struggling to stay balanced on the branch they were standing on, which kept swaying up and down, back and forth. They had their backs to me, so they were unaware that I had arrived. I didn't want to scare them, so I remained very still and quiet, watching them from behind. They looked like the best of friends sitting there, leaning on each other. It was the sweetest thing I had ever seen. This was the first time I had seen them sit this close since they were in the basket nest. The two of them sat as close as they could while trying to balance on the moving branch. Their fluffy feathers were blowing all over from the strong winds. It took a few minutes before one of them noticed me and turned around, as if to say hello. I don't think they heard me arrive, due to the howling of the wind and the noise of rustling leaves. Shortly after, the other sibling finally noticed me. With both owls now facing me, I could finally get a good look at them, side by side. I could clearly see it was Wisdom sitting on the left and Willow, who was still slightly smaller, sitting on the right. It was so great, finally making the distinction between the two of them. Also, I could now see how much they had grown and how far they both had come. The bond they had was incredible to see in the wild. I continued watching them for a while, noticing that Willow had almost caught up to Wisdom in size, but still appeared to be a little timid. Unlike his brother who still gave that strong stare, showing much more confidence as he stood by Willow's side. There was no mistaking the two of them, and they were both amazingly beautiful. After a while, Wisdom flew off to another tree, leaving Willow sitting on the branch alone. By himself, I could tell he was not as confident as his older sibling, but he was getting much better. I could see the strength building in his eyes, almost like he was trying to tell me, "See, I can do this!" He sat on the branch, watching me for a few more minutes, then he flew off to join Wisdom. I caught a glimpse of Mama sitting on a branch, way off in the distance. I didn't see Papa, but with no mess of feathers or fur in sight, I was confident the family was safe. I whispered goodbye and returned home myself.

65

Wisdom and Willow sitting close together on a tree limb.

Photograph by Cheryl Aguiar.

Wisdom noticed I had arrived.

Photograph by Cheryl Aguiar.

9

Nature's Way

OVER THE NEXT FEW WEEKS, I began noticing a change in both the owls, and their beautiful lush, wetland habitat. The early summer weather had differed dramatically from the cold, windy winter and the rainy spring we experienced earlier in the year. In fact, we had very little rain at all, unlike the weeks of non-stop rain while Wisdom and Willow were in the basket nest. With no rain, the stream which supplied the owls with many different sources of food was beginning to dry up. Without the water, there was less prey for the owl family to hunt. With less prey, that meant less food. I noticed the owls were moving farther into the woods where the tree canopy was thicker, and the stream had more water. I figured they had probably eaten everything that was left in what little water remained in the murky stream. It was getting tougher to spot them as they moved deeper into the thick foliage. My visits to the woods became shorter and shorter as time went on. I would always feel better if I caught a glimpse of at least one of them when I arrived. Sometimes,

I wouldn't see them at all, but a fallen feather would always let me know they were doing well. Most of the time, even if I couldn't see them in the trees, I would hear their screeches off in the distance; that was always a comforting sound.

By late June, the once plentiful stream had dried up completely. No rain had fallen in weeks. Tall grass and shrubs had begun to grow in the muddy, dried-up stream bed. I was hoping soon, we would get some much-needed rain to help fill the stream for my friends. I was beginning to see less and less of the owl family. One time, I saw one of the youngster's way off in the distance, sitting in a tree alongside the empty stream. He appeared to be all by himself, crying out for Mama. I looked in the surrounding trees, but she was nowhere in sight. That visit, I experienced a strange feeling inside; my heart ached with deep sadness as I watched him sitting alone. He stood for a little while longer, then flew off deeper into the woods. After a few minutes, I lost sight of him completely. Since I couldn't hear or see any of the others, I decided to return home; leaving with that empty feeling inside as if I might never see them again.

The next visit, I experienced an eerie silence in the woods. I saw nothing and heard nothing. Usually, I would hear at least one of them screeching from somewhere, but this time, no faint screeches off in the distance. My owl friends were nowhere to be found. I walked through the empty woods, looking around, thinking back to the times when they were there, hiding underneath the lush greens. I was sadly disappointed that I could not see them, but even worse than that... no feathers. I knew in an instant that my friends had moved on. Mama and Papa must have known it was time to leave the stream, taking the youngsters with them. They needed to go where they could find more food; survival is everything. I stayed for a little while longer, then headed home. I was still grateful for the chance to have spent so much time with them. I tried to remain hopeful, returning every few days to see if they had returned, but... nothing. I did not see or hear them at all.

Two weeks passed with still no sign of my friends. I called out to them with heartfelt wishes for some kind of sign that they were doing okay. Then finally one night, it rained! It was very little rain, not nearly enough to fill the stream, but it was sure a good sign. I couldn't wait to visit the woods to see if my friends had returned. As I entered the woods listening for their screeches, I was sadly disappointed again by the deafening silence. I stood looking and listening, but again... nothing. As I walked deeper into the woods, I could see something on top of the ferns. As I got closer, I was pleasantly surprised to see two beautiful feathers laid perfectly atop the ferns as if they had floated down from the sky. In my heart I knew, this was my sign. One of the feathers was a little smaller and lighter in color just like Willow. I instantly felt a sense of relief. One feather was from Willow and the other from Wisdom. I smiled now knowing, they were safe and sound. I looked up towards the trees, thanking my friends for the wonderful gifts. They had to have been there shortly before I arrived because the feathers would not have remained on top of the ferns after the rain we had earlier. They would have been soaking wet, dirty and matted to the ground, but they weren't. They were perfectly dry. I wondered if they had returned to see if the stream retained any of the rain water or maybe it was just to let me know they were all safe and doing well... again. It was amazing how every time I would start to lose hope, they were there. Whatever the reason, I was relieved to know they were okay and still close by. My guess was, Mama and Papa needed to bring them somewhere they could find more food. Without the stream, I'm sure all the animals that made a home there needed to move on to find food. It's the way of nature. I just hoped the owl family wouldn't travel too far away. I hoped to see them again someday soon. The stream had been the perfect home for them until it completely dried up, now they had ventured out beyond the safety of the well-hidden stream in search of the perfect place to call home.

An owl's territory can be up to three miles wide. It could be that the young owls had reached the age where they needed to explore new territories. Of course, I would have loved for them to stay in those woods, living in the three or four trees by the edge of the stream forever, but that was just not possible. Remember that famous saying I repeated to myself time and time again, "They are wild animals, and this is what they do."

Mama and Papa chose to stay by the stream while their fledglings were still young, keeping them well hidden and well fed. Now that they have grown, they need even more food and are old enough to travel longer distances. They can now travel with their parents to search for prey. Mama and Papa will continue feeding them until they learn to hunt for themselves. I can only hope they will return one day, after the rain has replenished the stream, bringing back the frogs, rats, snakes and other small animals. I will continue visiting the stream in hopes to see my friends again. Maybe they will leave a feather as a way of letting me know they are here, thriving and doing well.

Feather gifts from the owls. The bottom two on the right were the last two found on top of the ferns.

Photograph by Cheryl Aguiar.

We will watch for them in the tree tops surrounding us and listen for their screeching cries at dusk as they fly from tree to tree, waiting for food. That is a sound I will never forget. I will be waiting to hear Mama and Papa's hoots come fall, as this is the season owls start searching for new nests and begin roosting again. I was able to learn so much about them, having this opportunity to watch this family grow in the wild. I have become fascinated with these beautiful birds and will continue to learn more about them as time goes on. I will be forever grateful to have spent such precious time with this owl family.

One of the wonderful things about owls is, they mate for life. I am hopeful to see if Mama and Papa will return to add more siblings to the family next year! They usually will roost somewhere within their territory, then come January, begin nesting again. If owls have success raising their family, they will sometimes reuse the same nest the following year. I hope they pick a much better nest this time, but I will certainly be there to help if necessary! Wisdom and Willow will soon have to find mates and search for new territories of their own. (We have plenty of woods around us guys!) I hope they will all stay close; I wouldn't want to see any of them go far away. We hope to hear lots of echoing hoots from our friends throughout the fall and winter. Unlike most bird species who start singing their songs in early spring, owls become vocal in late fall and the early winter months. It is great to know that we now have four beautiful Great Horned Owls in our area instead of just two. We hope their families will continue to grow with each generation, as they will always be welcome here in our woods.

In my story, I refer to the youngsters as males, but I do not know the actual gender of my two little friends. If I had to guess, I would say Wisdom was a male and Willow was a female, but I could be wrong! As adults, the female is larger than the male! That distinction could not be made until these little guys were fully grown. Even then, it is sometimes hard to tell. Who knows, maybe I will get to find out someday. I will always be watching and listening for my owl friends and their families.

This was truly an amazing experience. I am grateful for the advice I was given from Mark on how to properly handle this situation as to not injury myself or the owls. I would advise anyone to seek professional help before handling any situation like this yourself. Wild animals can be very dangerous if not handled properly. My experience with this family was unique. Always use caution when approaching any wild animal that you see in your yard. Owl fledglings sometimes wander into yards before learning to fly. Unless you are sure the owl is injured or is too young to be out of the nest, the best thing you can do for them is to leave them alone. If you are not sure, please seek professional help. This will help protect you, the owls or any other wild animal you may encounter near your home. Be mindful of the animal and yourself, it will benefit you both.

I am so very grateful for the chance we were given to save these little owlets and the gift I received to watch them grow. Mama and Papa showed their gratitude by allowing me into their world. I will be forever changed by this once in a lifetime experience. I can only hope to see my owl friends again someday. Until then, may they fly free....

TWO MONTHS LATER

ON THE NIGHT OF AUGUST 31, 2016 at approximately 10:30 pm, the most amazing thing happened. It all started when Jim took a walk out to the barn in our backyard, where he keeps his truck. He had been charging the battery in his truck and went out to check on the progress. Just minutes after he went out, he came back to the house asking me, "What kind of sound do your owls make?" I stopped in my tracks with a long pause and said, "Why do you ask?" He then replied, "I think you need to come outside." He told me to walk very slowly out to the barn in the backyard. It was quite dark, but I continued walking, wondering what I was about to find. As I walked into the barn, I paused, listening carefully, but did not hear anything. "What did you hear?" I asked. He didn't answer right away, then replied, "Walk outside, behind the barn, towards the woods." As I walked behind the barn, I instantly heard a loud screech from the trees right at the edge of the woods. I turned around quickly, almost knocking Jim over, I whispered with excitement "That's my baby! That's one of the little owls!" He was sitting up in the tree right in front of us. We couldn't see him in the dark, but we could certainly hear him. I knew that sound anywhere. Jim said the screech scared the daylights out of him when he first entered the barn; he actually jumped the first time he heard it. After hearing the screech three times, he said to himself, "What the heck is that? Hmmm, I wonder if that could be an owl? It has to be!" He came to get me right away. I had told him about their screeches before, but until now he had never heard them.

I could not believe what I was hearing. I only heard one of the young owls, but I was so excited! "Hello little guy! Where have you been?" I said. Jim and I tried to spot his silhouette in the light from the moon, but we could not see him. Just like before, I didn't even care that I couldn't see him; just knowing he was alive and well was enough for me. I whispered to him, "You came to tell me that you were all right, didn't you? Thank you, little guy, I was so worried!" I stayed outside for a while just listening to him screech. Oh, how I missed that sound. I had been looking in those trees every time I went outside for the last two months. I also visited the stream a couple of times a week hoping I would see or hear my little friends but always found an empty, silent woods. Now, he came to me. The sound I had been longing to hear was coming from my own backyard.

The next night I went outside at dusk, excited to see if my friend was still in the woods. Not only was he still there, but much to my surprise… I heard two separate screeches! Wisdom and Willow were both there, right in my own woods. This was so incredible. If only, I could have seen them. I tried so hard to locate them, but it gets very dark in those woods and they hide so well. I stood listening to the two of them screech back and forth until bedtime. This continued every night for the next two weeks. My friends had returned to their original home. I was so happy they felt comfortable enough to come back here. They were not frightened away by the human interaction after all. Perhaps they felt this was the safest place to be. I would always be here to help if they need me! I'm sure Mama and Papa were around somewhere although I did not see or hear them. It could have been that they stopped feeding Wisdom and Willow at that point, forcing them to fend for themselves. It will soon be time for the little guys to go off on their own. Mama and Papa will encourage them to hunt by feeding them less and less as time goes on. The youngster's loud screeches are actually cries for food. They are begging their parents to feed them. It was so sad to hear them beg, but this is how they learn. Eventually, they will get hungry enough to try hunting on their own. Everything was going just as it should.

About two weeks later, we stopped hearing the screeches from our little friends. I hoped that meant they had finally started hunting on their own. Jim and I were getting ready to leave for a two-week road trip to the mountains, so I asked my mother to keep watch and listen for them while I was gone. Unfortunately, she did not hear them at all. When we returned home from our trip, I immediately went out back calling to them, "Hi guys, I'm home! I hope you are all doing okay out there!" I didn't hear any screeching, so I went back in for the night.

The next night, my other neighbor Celeste, who I had been keeping updated on the progress of this owl family every step of the way, called and said she heard something screeching in the woods behind our homes. I instantly grabbed my coat, a flashlight and ran outside to meet her. As soon as I stepped into the woods, I heard one of the little guys. I said, "Hello little guy, I'm so glad you're here!" I continued walking through the woods to meet Celeste. I was happy to tell her that the sound she was hearing, was indeed Wisdom or Willow. She finally had a chance to hear the screech from one of the little owls we all loved so dearly. Again, we could not see him, but both agreed, hearing him was all we cared about. Just knowing he was there was so amazing. We listened for a while, then I returned home to tell Jim the great news. I was so excited to hear one of them and could only hope the rest of the family was safe too. Maybe, the next sounds we hear from the little guys will be actual hoots!

Either way, I know they are here, safe and well on their way to becoming the magnificent adult Great Horned Owls that I hoped they would be. I'm sure they will be just fine, besides, Mama and Papa need to start looking for a new nest to start all over again. It will be exciting to see what the winter months will bring for this entire owl family. I am hoping for many more years to watch and learn from these precious owls. By working together and respecting nature, we kept the family safe, giving them the chance to succeed. They all showed amazing strength and will, justifying the statement… **Where There's a Will, There's a Way.**

~ Cheryl Aguiar

Who Knows What Tomorrow May Bring....

View more pictures or purchase prints at:

www.roadsidestills.com

See Gallery: Great Horned Owlets Rescue Pictures

ABOUT THE AUTHOR

CHERYL AGUIAR is a first-time author and entrepreneur who has an intuitive admiration and in-depth respect for nature and its wildlife.

Cheryl is a hardworking, self-employed salon owner in the small, New England Town of Westport, Massachusetts where she also resides with her husband Jim. Cheryl and Jim live in a quaint, country style home, hand built by themselves near the woods she explored as a child. With nothing more than a high school diploma, Cheryl has succeeded in her businesses, becoming a self-taught photographer and learning the art of writing.

Cheryl's true passion is her love for nature, traveling, exploring and photographing the beauty of our landscapes and magnificent wildlife all around the country. She travels whenever it's possible with her husband Jim. They also own land in New Vineyard, Maine, their own piece of woodland paradise. In discovering the amazing beauty surrounding her homes and around the country, Cheryl founded Roadside Stills Photography and continues growing while exploring her talents. Her strong passion and entrepreneurial spirit have granted her the ability to share her experiences with nature through the lens of a camera and now… on paper.

Made in the USA
Lexington, KY
05 December 2018